ISBN:
978-0-578-98498-8

SOCIAL MEDIA
PLANNER

The 52-Week Social Media Content Planner For Your Business

IT'S YOUR TIME

We can't avoid social media. Just as you want to reject it, official Tweets are being read on the news, and media interviews of experts are preceded by an introduction listing the expert's TikTok stats. 12 million followers? 50 million views?

It's your time to have a strong presence on each of the top platforms, where consumers search daily for content that keeps them interested or motivates them to engage. When we say engage, we mean any action they take with your post—share it, comment on it, post an emoji reacting to it, rewatch it, save it for future reference, use it as a basis for a new post of their own, or the classic: love it/upvote it. Any action social media users take with your post can increase the number of views that it gets, as it gets shared to those users' friends and followers, potentially getting you more engagement from users that were never followers of your page, people that didn't know about your brand/business, or people who forgot it exists.

Even if you're already posting on social media successfully, but need organization or can't get a steady rhythm going -- or if you're thinking about posting for your business on social media to seem reputable, but don't know which content is right for you, this planner is going to be your guide toward managing your social media. While posting about your business 52 weeks in a row, you're bound to go on a journey of rediscovering everything that's great and exciting about your business, and you'll learn about what speaks to your online followers and clientele.

It's your time to say, "yes! Follow me @_______" instead of "Oh, I don't do social media" or "my business doesn't do Facebook."

"I JUST post on Facebook! I don't like the others!"

Even though we, on average, pick up our cell phones every 12 minutes, we don't all pick up the phone to go to Facebook only… or to go only to Instagram. There are many who may be like you, and have a preference for their social media, and if your business is not appearing on that platform, you are missing potential customers every single day.

TWITTER is a great example. The number of people searching on Twitter everyday is 1.6 billion and guess what? Not all of them have accounts. That's right. Even people that don't tweet, read tweets, and those are potential leads for your business, if you're positioning your content regularly.

As you get familiar with each platform below, think about it in the context of your business.

TWITTER

Get on Twitter. It doesn't matter if you don't know how. Steps to follow are easy found online.
Please create an account, even if it's just a test, so you can learn this steps with me. Imagine we're going to a networking event, where everybody's talking when we arrive. Some people have had one too many, some people are lost, some people are all hovering over in a section. Who do we greet first? Everything they're saying are "tweets." The pool of conversations at the event are searchable. The event is right now. When you search, you also see the #trending part, which is where everyone is hovering. The hashtags are "search terms" without spaces. #LosAngeles or a fact about product you're selling #nowinstock. Or it can be more general about how you're feeling #motivated or what you're offering #motivating #essentialoils #emergencyplumber
People at the networking event talk back and forth by replying to each other's tweets. If, based on their content, you like a business or a person enough to follow them, you can log in and always see that account's tweets.

FACEBOOK

Unavoidable and cliché, but so important for your business. You have to embrace it and participate in conversations with your followers. The good thing is that with a business page, you can aim to steer clear of the controversial posts, and that way, be among today's crowd, but only there for positive vibes. It's a huge crowd. There are 2.89 billion active users and people search 2 billion queries on Facebook every day.
One huge benefit from having a business page is the validation you get from being pereceived as a reputable business that is on Facebook, that does post, and is consistent.
Facebook reviews are almost as important as Google reviews these days, and I would encourage you to value both and provide your customers the option of leaving you reviews on Facebook more and more each day. Those reviews actually get picked up by Google, and will display in the search results, so you give potential leads that find you in searches the opportunity to read your reviews

INSTAGRAM

Think of Instagram as your second storefront, whether you sell inventory or provide a service. Accounts can post their highlight reel or they can show vulnerabilities and uniquenesses. Here, hashtags are the conversation starters, and again, these are searchable terms without spaces that you can type in the search bar at the top when you log in to social media to find what people are posting about, or what this moment's Instagram conversations are about. Throughout the weeks, you will post signage like you would at a brick and mortar location. Instead of foot traffic, there's online traffick, which you do want. Here, you have the option to also post video, which is huge. Not only videos that your viewers can watch wenever, but also videos that are your "Reels," which let you explore with your brand and be active on social media everyday. On Instagram, your page also should follow an aesthetic -- something consistent in your photos/videos/captions that expresses the personality of a brand. This can change per season with new arrivals, or with color schemes, or with the angles from which you shoot your inventory. Incentives and contests are also something you can run through your Instagram to entice your followers to develop a relationship with you, and engage with your store as you post. If users like a product enough to purchase it, they're directed to a link to your website (your main online storefront, with more inventory and online payment options.

PINTREST

Let's pretend we have a lot of cork boards and we want other people to see what we post on them. It doesn't matter if you're not into arts and crafts. The boards could be full of ideas, of things that inspire your business, or of currently/future products, themes—anything you would hang on a display. Each cork board has it's own name or title. This is searchable by other people, who also have cork boards, and who want you to see what they have. There are currently 478 million monthly active users. The pictures or videos you post are your "pins." If users want, they can pin your pin to their "board." You post your pins to the appropriate "boards" you share. Users search for titles or names of other people's boards when they search for "interests," which is why you want to pick a searchable name for each of your corkboards.

SNAPCHAT

It's sensational in the moment, and then it's gone. With Snapchat you want whoever's listening to hear this/to watch this/to see you with a "filter" or fun face alterations right now, or not to see it at all. On the app, you can make videos that are seen by people searching for public "snaps" or videos in your area, and that way attract local leads to your content, then your profile, then your website, and hopefully leading to conversions, and then to sales. Do not miss this moment. What's that instant? Sale today at 5 pm. New artist featured in tonight's line up. The material of these sweaters is unbelievably soft. 293 million daily active users worldwide could be watching, so make content with a touch of spontaneity and more freedom to engage right now with your public.

TIKTOK

TikTok is not just a dance party. There are so many niche categories or hashtags that you can search for, and the content really keeps users engaged, so much so, that the app has over 20 billion downloads worldwide, and it was the most downloaded app in 2020. Android users, for example, spend an average of 13.3 hours a month on TikTok, and your business' content could be among the videos people like, comment on, reply to with a video, or share with their friends. In this platform, you really want to provide useful/entertaining/engaging content, in short snippets. Include audio in the sound, occasional graphics, and the greatest part is that the platform lets you make all these video enhancements and edits directly when posting a TikTok video. Share interesting topics about your industry, give your opinion that shows your authority in your field, give people solutions that they would find helpful, and then get the opportunity of users going to your profile, clicking your website, and becoming ambassadors and clients of your business. Did you just get a new shipment? Make a video unloading the trucks and hype up the release of the new inventory. Know an easy plumbing fix for clogged sinks at home? Show users DIY fixes so they get to know your business to potentially hire you for more complex problems they experience.

HELP SHAPE PUBLIC OPINION

Something exciting about creating content is the idea that you're creating the future that people will get to see published as you decide. It's your call. You know that you have a voice to put out there since you bought or were gifted this planner, and within it you'll develop unbelievable growth is many ways. Look, I recognize that you know that you excel at your specialty and you're truly an expert in your industry. If you trust this journey, you'll develop - week by week - to connect the dots that are revealed through repetition and analysis of one's behavior; in this case, posting week by week. All of these are quantifiable in your new social media planner, so you can make data-driven decisions.

Facbook Prompts- See your business from different angles, fall in love again with your business, learn 52 quotable facts about your business over this year.

Instagram Prompts- plan out your photography and inspiration to understand how your business can be represented visually every day.

Pintrest Posts- Share past and current inpiring things going on in the business or that represent your business' value weekly, along with links to where users can find more information. Your website is a good idea to use as the link because they will get to engage more with your brand.

Snapchat Breakdown- Discover moments of your day that you should share, and plan out when you'll make those moments available for 24 hours.

Twitter Prompts- Don't be afraid to quote yourself. Snippets of your bussiness' daily "behind-the-scenes" are good ways to lead good conversations throughout the next year.

TikTok Videos- Plan out your photography and inspiration to understand how your business can be represented visually every day.

All skills take practice, and as long as you follow the 52 week comitment, your online audience demands, you'll see that social media is manageable by you. To begin, have an open mind.

Board Name S/M

Add your title

Describe your pin

Your website

Board Name T/W

Add your title

Describe your pin

Your website

Your Account
Monday
Post about your company

Your Account
Tuesday
Post about a product/service

Your Account
Wednesday
Post about your industry

Ideas:

Your Account
Sunday
Post a link to a blog or person you respect & your opinion

Your Account
Thursday
Post about your staff

Your Account
Friday
Post about your business logo & info

Your Account
Saturday
Post your opinion on a trending topic

Ideas:

Business Picture
Monday

Behind the scenes clip
Tuesday

Branding Visual
Wednesday

Product/Service
Thursday

Industry Trivia/Fact
Friday

Featured Review
Saturday

Industry FAQ
Sunday

Reel
______

M ____________________

T ____________________

W ____________________

T ____________________

F ____________________

S ____________________

S ____________________

TikTok users want to co-create content based on a TikTok you post. Say something thought provoking!

Dates: ______________________________

Board Name T/F

Add your title

Describe your pin

Your website

Board Name S

Add your title

Describe your pin

Your website

Mon

Tweet about your company

Tues

Tweet about a product/service

Wed

Tweet highlighting one of your online reviews

Thurs

Tweet about your industry

Fri

Tweet about something trending this week

Sat

Tweet about an upcoming sale or season

Sun

Tweet an answer to an FAQ in your industry

Weekly Hashtags ______________________________

Industry News ______________________________

Weekly Winners: MOST COMMENTS: LIKES: SHARES:

Board Name S/M

Add your title

Describe your pin

Your website

Board Name T/W

Add your title

Describe your pin

Your website

Your Account
Monday
Post about a your company

Your Account
Tuesday
Post about a product/service

Your Account
Wednesday
Post about your industry

Your Account
Thursday
Post about your staff

Your Account
Friday
Post about your business logo & info

Your Account
Saturday
Post your opinion on a trending topic

Ideas:

Your Account
Sunday
Post a link to a blog or person you respect & your opinion

Ideas:

Business Picture
Monday

Behind the scenes clip
Tuesday

Branding Visual
Wednesday

Product/Service
Thursday

Industry Trivia/Fact
Friday

Featured Review
Saturday

Industry FAQ
Sunday

Reel
______

M ________________________

T ________________________

W ________________________

T ________________________

F ________________________

S ________________________

S ________________________

Average users spent 2 hours and 24 minutes per day on social media in 2020.

Dates: ______________________

Board Name T/F

Add your title

Describe your pin

Your website

Board Name S

Add your title

Describe your pin

Your website

Mon

Tweet about your company

Tues

Tweet about a product/service

Wed

Tweet highlighting one of your online reviews

Thurs

Tweet about your industry

Fri

Tweet about something trending this week

Sat

Tweet about an upcoming sale or season

Sun

Tweet an answer to an FAQ in your industry

Weekly Hashtags ______________________

Industry News ______________________

Weekly Winners: MOST COMMENTS: LIKES: SHARES:

Board Name S/M

Add your title

Describe your pin

Your website

Board Name T/W

Add your title

Describe your pin

Your website

Your Account
Monday
Post about a your company

Your Account
Tuesday
Post about a product/service

Your Account
Wednesday
Post about your industry

Ideas:

Your Account
Sunday
Post a link to a blog or person you respect & your opinion

Your Account
Thursday
Post about your staff

Your Account
Friday
Post about your business logo & info

Your Account
Saturday
Post your opinion on a trending topic

Ideas:

Business Picture
Monday

Behind the scenes clip
Tuesday

Branding Visual
Wednesday

Product/Service
Thursday

M ____________________

T ____________________

W ____________________

T ____________________

F ____________________

S ____________________

S ____________________

Industry Trivia/Fact
Friday

Featured Review
Saturday

Industry FAQ
Sunday

Reel
______

People spend an average of 2 hours and 24 minutes each day on Facebook. Make sure you're there.

Dates: ____________________

Board Name T/F

Add your title

Describe your pin

Your website

Board Name S

Add your title

Describe your pin

Your website

Mon

Tweet about your company

Tues

Tweet about a product/service

Wed

Tweet highlighting one of your online reviews

Thurs

Tweet about your industry

Fri

Tweet about something trending this week

Sat

Tweet about an upcoming sale or season

Sun

Tweet an answer to an FAQ in your industry

Weekly Hashtags ____________________

Industry News ____________________

Weekly Winners: MOST COMMENTS: LIKES: SHARES:

Board Name S/M

Add your title

Describe your pin

Your website

Board Name T/W

Add your title

Describe your pin

Your website

Your Account
Monday
Post about a your company

Your Account
Tuesday
Post about a product/service

Your Account
Wednesday
Post about your industry

Ideas:

Your Account
Sunday
Post a link to a blog or person you respect & your opinion

Your Account
Thursday
Post about your staff

Your Account
Friday
Post about your business logo & info

Your Account
Saturday
Post your opinion on a trending topic

Ideas:

Business Picture
Monday

Behind the scenes clip
Tuesday

Branding Visual
Wednesday

Product/Service
Thursday

Industry Trivia/Fact
Friday

Featured Review
Saturday

Industry FAQ
Sunday

Reel

M ____________________

T ____________________

W ____________________

T ____________________

F ____________________

S ____________________

S ____________________

On Pintrest, users will organize and tag your content, so your boards and pins should be titled with searchable terms.

Dates: ______________________________

Board Name T/F

Add your title

Describe your pin

Your website

Board Name S

Add your title

Describe your pin

Your website

Mon

Tweet about your company

Tues

Tweet about a product/service

Wed

Tweet highlighting one of your online reviews

Thurs

Tweet about your industry

Fri

Tweet about something trending this week

Sat

Tweet about an upcoming sale or season

Sun

Tweet an answer to an FAQ in your industry

Weekly Hashtags ______________________________

Industry News ______________________________

Weekly Winners: MOST COMMENTS: LIKES: SHARES:

Board Name S/M

Add your title

Describe your pin

Your website

Board Name T/W

Add your title

Describe your pin

Your website

Your Account
Monday
Post about a your company

Your Account
Tuesday
Post about a product/service

Your Account
Wednesday
Post about your industry

Ideas:

Your Account
Sunday
Post a link to a blog or person you respect & your opinion

Your Account
Thursday
Post about your staff

Your Account
Friday
Post about your business logo & info

Your Account
Saturday
Post your opinion on a trending topic

Ideas:

Business Picture
Monday

Behind the scenes clip
Tuesday

Branding Visual
Wednesday

Product/Service
Thursday

Industry Trivia/Fact
Friday

Featured Review
Saturday

Industry FAQ
Sunday

Reel
______

M ________________________

T ________________________

W ________________________

T ________________________

F ________________________

S ________________________

S ________________________

82% of the audiences prefer live videos on social media, so go live on Facebook, TikTok, or Twitter, Snapchat, Pintrest or Instagram!

Dates: ____________________

Board Name T/F

Add your title

Describe your pin

Your website

Board Name S

Add your title

Describe your pin

Your website

Mon

Tweet about your company

Tues

Tweet about a product/service

Wed

Tweet highlighting one of your online reviews

Thurs

Tweet about your industry

Fri

Tweet about something trending this week

Sat

Tweet about an upcoming sale or season

Sun

Tweet an answer to an FAQ in your industry

Weekly Hashtags ____________________

Industry News ____________________

Weekly Winners: MOST COMMENTS: LIKES: SHARES: ____________________

Board Name S/M

Add your title

Describe your pin

Your website

Board Name T/W

Add your title

Describe your pin

Your website

Your Account
Monday
Post about a your company

Your Account
Tuesday
Post about a product/service

Your Account
Wednesday
Post about your industry

Ideas:

Your Account
Sunday
Post a link to a blog or person you respect & your opinion

Your Account
Thursday
Post about your staff

Your Account
Friday
Post about your business logo & info

Your Account
Saturday
Post your opinion on a trending topic

Ideas:

Business Picture
Monday

Behind the scenes clip
Tuesday

Branding Visual
Wednesday

Product/Service
Thursday

Industry Trivia/Fact
Friday

Featured Review
Saturday

Industry FAQ
Sunday

Reel
______

M ______________________________

T ______________________________

W ______________________________

T ______________________________

F ______________________________

S ______________________________

S ______________________________

____

____

____

____

Instagram brand stories are aimed to be more personal and informal so give customers a sneak peek into your company's world!

Dates: ______________________________

Board Name T/F

Add your title

Describe your pin

Your website

Board Name S

Add your title

Describe your pin

Your website

Mon

Tweet about your company

Tues

Tweet about a product/service

Wed

Tweet highlighting one of your online reviews

Thurs

Tweet about your industry

Fri

Tweet about something trending this week

Sat

Tweet about an upcoming sale or season

Sun

Tweet an answer to an FAQ in your industry

Weekly Hashtags ______________________________

Industry News ______________________________

Weekly Winners: MOST COMMENTS: LIKES: SHARES:

Board Name S/M

Add your title

Describe your pin

Your website

Board Name T/W

Add your title

Describe your pin

Your website

Your Account
Monday
Post about a your company

Your Account
Tuesday
Post about a product/service

Your Account
Wednesday
Post about your industry

Ideas:

Your Account
Sunday
Post a link to a blog or person you respect & your opinion

Your Account
Thursday
Post about your staff

Your Account
Friday
Post about your business logo & info

Your Account
Saturday
Post your opinion on a trending topic

Ideas:

Business Picture
Monday

Behind the scenes clip
Tuesday

Branding Visual
Wednesday

Product/Service
Thursday

Industry Trivia/Fact
Friday

Featured Review
Saturday

Industry FAQ
Sunday

Reel
______

M ______________________

T ______________________

W ______________________

T ______________________

F ______________________

S ______________________

S ______________________

____

____

____

____

Tagging your location on Instagram, Snapchat, and Facebook will allow you to be discovered locally by social media users in your vicinity.

Dates: ______________________________

Board Name T/F

Add your title

Describe your pin

Your website

Board Name S

Add your title

Describe your pin

Your website

Mon

Tweet about your company

Tues

Tweet about a product/service

Wed

Tweet highlighting one of your online reviews

Thurs

Tweet about your industry

Fri

Tweet about something trending this week

Sat

Tweet about an upcoming sale or season

Sun

Tweet an answer to an FAQ in your industry

Weekly Hashtags ______________________________

Industry News ______________________________

Weekly Winners: MOST COMMENTS: LIKES: SHARES:

Board Name S/M

Add your title

Describe your pin

Your website

Board Name T/W

Add your title

Describe your pin

Your website

Your Account
Monday
Post about a your company

Your Account
Tuesday
Post about a product/service

Your Account
Wednesday
Post about your industry

Ideas:

Your Account
Sunday
Post a link to a blog or person you respect & your opinion

Your Account
Thursday
Post about your staff

Your Account
Friday
Post about your business logo & info

Your Account
Saturday
Post your opinion on a trending topic

Ideas:

Business Picture
Monday

Behind the scenes clip
Tuesday

Branding Visual
Wednesday

Product/Service
Thursday

Industry Trivia/Fact
Friday

Featured Review
Saturday

Industry FAQ
Sunday

Reel
______

M ______________________

T ______________________

W ______________________

T ______________________

F ______________________

S ______________________

S ______________________

____

____

____

____

Many influencers will post your product if you send them the product, and this can gain you sales, which are quantifiable if you issue your influencer a discount code that lets you know when their followers purchased your product.

Dates: ______________________

Board Name T/F

Add your title

Describe your pin

Your website

Board Name S

Add your title

Describe your pin

Your website

Mon

Tweet about your company

Tues

Tweet about a product/service

Wed

Tweet highlighting one of your online reviews

Thurs

Tweet about your industry

Fri

Tweet about something trending this week

Sat

Tweet about an upcoming sale or season

Sun

Tweet an answer to an FAQ in your industry

Weekly Hashtags ______________________

Industry News ______________________

Weekly Winners: MOST COMMENTS: LIKES: SHARES:

Board Name S/M

Add your title

Describe your pin

Your website

Board Name T/W

Add your title

Describe your pin

Your website

Your Account
Monday
Post about a your company

Your Account
Tuesday
Post about a product/service

Your Account
Wednesday
Post about your industry

Ideas:

Your Account
Sunday
Post a link to a blog or person you respect & your opinion

Your Account
Thursday
Post about your staff

Your Account
Friday
Post about your business logo & info

Your Account
Saturday
Post your opinion on a trending topic

Ideas:

Business Picture
Monday

Behind the scenes clip
Tuesday

Branding Visual
Wednesday

Product/Service
Thursday

Industry Trivia/Fact
Friday

Featured Review
Saturday

Industry FAQ
Sunday

Reel
______

M ______________________________

T ______________________________

W ______________________________

T ______________________________

F ______________________________

S ______________________________

S ______________________________

Treat your customers as if they're all influencers. Make sure they have the best experience with your business that will be worth sharing with their friends.

Dates: ______________________

Board Name T/F

Add your title

Describe your pin

Your website

Board Name S

Add your title

Describe your pin

Your website

Mon

Tweet about your company

Tues

Tweet about a product/service

Wed

Tweet highlighting one of your online reviews

Thurs

Tweet about your industry

Fri

Tweet about something trending this week

Sat

Tweet about an upcoming sale or season

Sun

Tweet an answer to an FAQ in your industry

Weekly Hashtags ______________________

Industry News ______________________

Weekly Winners: MOST COMMENTS: LIKES: SHARES:

Board Name S/M

Add your title

Describe your pin

Your website

Board Name T/W

Add your title

Describe your pin

Your website

Your Account
Monday
Post about a your company

Your Account
Tuesday
Post about a product/service

Your Account
Wednesday
Post about your industry

Ideas:

Your Account
Sunday
Post a link to a blog or person you respect & your opinion

Your Account
Thursday
Post about your staff

Your Account
Friday
Post about your business logo & info

Your Account
Saturday
Post your opinion on a trending topic

Ideas:

Business Picture
Monday

Behind the scenes clip
Tuesday

Branding Visual
Wednesday

Product/Service
Thursday

M ______

T ______

W ______

T ______

F ______

S ______

S ______

Industry Trivia/Fact
Friday

Featured Review
Saturday

Industry FAQ
Sunday

Reel

Videos grab the attention of users and keep them hooked on the screen, so make sure your opening visual, sound or voice are compelling.

Dates: ______________________________

Board Name T/F

Add your title

Describe your pin

Your website

Board Name S

Add your title

Describe your pin

Your website

Mon

Tweet about your company

Tues

Tweet about a product/service

Wed

Tweet highlighting one of your online reviews

Thurs

Tweet about your industry

Fri

Tweet about something trending this week

Sat

Tweet about an upcoming sale or season

Sun

Tweet an answer to an FAQ in your industry

Weekly Hashtags ______________________________

Industry News ______________________________

Weekly Winners: MOST COMMENTS: LIKES: SHARES: ______________________________

Board Name S/M

Add your title

Describe your pin

Your website

Board Name T/W

Add your title

Describe your pin

Your website

Your Account
Monday
Post about a your company

Your Account
Tuesday
Post about a product/service

Your Account
Wednesday
Post about your industry

Ideas:

Your Account
Sunday
Post a link to a blog or person you respect & your opinion

Your Account
Thursday
Post about your staff

Your Account
Friday
Post about your business logo & info

Your Account
Saturday
Post your opinion on a trending topic

Ideas:

Business Picture
Monday

Behind the scenes clip
Tuesday

Branding Visual
Wednesday

Product/Service
Thursday

M ______

T ______

W ______

T ______

F ______

S ______

S ______

Industry Trivia/Fact
Friday

Featured Review
Saturday

Industry FAQ
Sunday

Reel
______

TikTok is used by 21% of Americans, which is roughly 6,997,5126 people.

Dates: ______________________________

Board Name T/F

Add your title

Describe your pin

Your website

Board Name S

Add your title

Describe your pin

Your website

Mon

Tweet about your company

Tues

Tweet about a product/service

Wed

Tweet highlighting one of your online reviews

Thurs

Tweet about your industry

Fri

Tweet about something trending this week

Sat

Tweet about an upcoming sale or season

Sun

Tweet an answer to an FAQ in your industry

Weekly Hashtags ______________________________

Industry News ______________________________

Weekly Winners: MOST COMMENTS: LIKES: SHARES:

Board Name S/M

Add your title

Describe your pin

Your website

Board Name T/W

Add your title

Describe your pin

Your website

Your Account
Monday
Post about a your company

Your Account
Tuesday
Post about a product/service

Your Account
Wednesday
Post about your industry

Ideas:

Your Account
Sunday
Post a link to a blog or person you respect & your opinion

Your Account
Thursday
Post about your staff

Your Account
Friday
Post about your business logo & info

Your Account
Saturday
Post your opinion on a trending topic

Ideas:

Business Picture
Monday

Behind the scenes clip
Tuesday

Branding Visual
Wednesday

Product/Service
Thursday

Industry Trivia/Fact
Friday

Featured Review
Saturday

Industry FAQ
Sunday

Reel
_____

M ________________

T ________________

W ________________

T ________________

F ________________

S ________________

S ________________

71 % of 18-29 year olds use Instagram

Dates: ______________________

Board Name T/F

Add your title

Describe your pin

Your website

Board Name S

Add your title

Describe your pin

Your website

Mon

Tweet about your company

Tues

Tweet about a product/service

Wed

Tweet highlighting one of your online reviews

Thurs

Tweet about your industry

Fri

Tweet about something trending this week

Sat

Tweet about an upcoming sale or season

Sun

Tweet an answer to an FAQ in your industry

Weekly Hashtags ______________________

Industry News ______________________

Weekly Winners: MOST COMMENTS: LIKES: SHARES: ______________________

Board Name S/M

Add your title

Describe your pin

Your website

Board Name T/W

Add your title

Describe your pin

Your website

Your Account
Monday
Post about a your company

Your Account
Tuesday
Post about a product/service

Your Account
Wednesday
Post about your industry

Ideas:

Your Account
Sunday
Post a link to a blog or person you respect & your opinion

Your Account
Thursday
Post about your staff

Your Account
Friday
Post about your business logo & info

Your Account
Saturday
Post your opinion on a trending topic

Ideas:

Business Picture
Monday

Behind the scenes clip
Tuesday

Branding Visual
Wednesday

Product/Service
Thursday

Industry Trivia/Fact
Friday

Featured Review
Saturday

Industry FAQ
Sunday

Reel
______

M ____________________

T ____________________

W ____________________

T ____________________

F ____________________

S ____________________

S ____________________

65% of adults 18-29 use Snapchat.

Dates: ____________________

Board Name T/F

Add your title

Describe your pin

Your website

Board Name S

Add your title

Describe your pin

Your website

Mon

Tweet about your company

Tues

Tweet about a product/service

Wed

Tweet highlighting one of your online reviews

Thurs

Tweet about your industry

Fri

Tweet about something trending this week

Sat

Tweet about an upcoming sale or season

Sun

Tweet an answer to an FAQ in your industry

Weekly Hashtags ____________________

Industry News ____________________

Weekly Winners: MOST COMMENTS: LIKES: SHARES:

Board Name S/M

Add your title

Describe your pin

Your website

Board Name T/W

Add your title

Describe your pin

Your website

Your Account
Monday
Post about a your company

Your Account
Tuesday
Post about a product/service

Your Account
Wednesday
Post about your industry

Ideas:

Your Account
Sunday
Post a link to a blog or person you respect & your opinion

Your Account
Thursday
Post about your staff

Your Account
Friday
Post about your business logo & info

Your Account
Saturday
Post your opinion on a trending topic

Ideas:

Business Picture
Monday

Behind the scenes clip
Tuesday

Branding Visual
Wednesday

Product/Service
Thursday

Industry Trivia/Fact
Friday

Featured Review
Saturday

Industry FAQ
Sunday

Reel

M

T

W

T

F

S

S

For every social channel you add, you can improve your ROI and effectiveness by up to 35%, according to Analytic Partners.

Dates: ______________________________

Board Name T/F

Add your title

Describe your pin

Your website

Board Name S

Add your title

Describe your pin

Your website

Mon

Tweet about your company

Tues

Tweet about a product/service

Wed

Tweet highlighting one of your online reviews

Thurs

Tweet about your industry

Fri

Tweet about something trending this week

Sat

Tweet about an upcoming sale or season

Sun

Tweet an answer to an FAQ in your industry

Weekly Hashtags ______________________________

Industry News ______________________________

Weekly Winners: MOST COMMENTS: LIKES: SHARES: ______________________________

Board Name S/M

Add your title

Describe your pin

Your website

Board Name T/W

Add your title

Describe your pin

Your website

Your Account
Monday
Post about a your company

Your Account
Tuesday
Post about a product/service

Your Account
Wednesday
Post about your industry

Ideas:

Your Account
Sunday
Post a link to a blog or person you respect & your opinion

Your Account
Thursday
Post about your staff

Your Account
Friday
Post about your business logo & info

Your Account
Saturday
Post your opinion on a trending topic

Ideas:

Business Picture
Monday

Behind the scenes clip
Tuesday

Branding Visual
Wednesday

Product/Service
Thursday

Industry Trivia/Fact
Friday

Featured Review
Saturday

Industry FAQ
Sunday

Reel
______

M ____________________

T ____________________

W ____________________

T ____________________

F ____________________

S ____________________

S ____________________

____

____

____

____

For businesses who don't invest in paid advertising, Twitter and Pinterest are seen as the most effective channels.

Dates: ______________________________

Board Name T/F

Add your title

Describe your pin

Your website

Board Name S

Add your title

Describe your pin

Your website

Mon

Tweet about your company

Tues

Tweet about a product/service

Wed

Tweet highlighting one of your online reviews

Thurs

Tweet about your industry

Fri

Tweet about something trending this week

Sat

Tweet about an upcoming sale or season

Sun

Tweet an answer to an FAQ in your industry

Weekly Hashtags ______________________________

Industry News ______________________________

Weekly Winners: MOST COMMENTS: LIKES: SHARES:

Board Name S/M

Add your title

Describe your pin

Your website

Board Name T/W

Add your title

Describe your pin

Your website

Your Account
Monday
Post about a your company

Your Account
Tuesday
Post about a product/service

Your Account
Wednesday
Post about your industry

Ideas:

Your Account
Sunday
Post a link to a blog or person you respect & your opinion

Your Account
Thursday
Post about your staff

Your Account
Friday
Post about your business logo & info

Your Account
Saturday
Post your opinion on a trending topic

Ideas:

Business Picture
Monday

Behind the scenes clip
Tuesday

Branding Visual
Wednesday

Product/Service
Thursday

Industry Trivia/Fact
Friday

Featured Review
Saturday

Industry FAQ
Sunday

Reel
______

M ____________________

T ____________________

W ____________________

T ____________________

F ____________________

S ____________________

S ____________________

____

____

____

____

More than 400 million people use Pintrest to find tomorrow's ideas. Give them ideas!

Dates: ______________________

Board Name T/F

Add your title

Describe your pin

Your website

Board Name S

Add your title

Describe your pin

Your website

Mon

- [ ] Tweet about your company

Tues

- [ ] Tweet about a product/service

Wed

- [ ] Tweet highlighting one of your online reviews

Thurs

- [ ] Tweet about your industry

Fri

- [ ] Tweet about something trending this week

Sat

- [ ] Tweet about an upcoming sale or season

Sun

- [ ] Tweet an answer to an FAQ in your industry

Weekly Hashtags ______________________

Industry News ______________________

Weekly Winners: MOST COMMENTS: LIKES: SHARES:

Board Name S/M

Add your title

Describe your pin

Your website

Board Name T/W

Add your title

Describe your pin

Your website

Your Account
Monday
Post about a your company

Your Account
Tuesday
Post about a product/service

Your Account
Wednesday
Post about your industry

Ideas:

Your Account
Sunday
Post a link to a blog or person you respect & your opinion

Your Account
Thursday
Post about your staff

Your Account
Friday
Post about your business logo & info

Your Account
Saturday
Post your opinion on a trending topic

Ideas:

Business Picture
Monday

Behind the scenes clip
Tuesday

Branding Visual
Wednesday

Product/Service
Thursday

Industry Trivia/Fact
Friday

Featured Review
Saturday

Industry FAQ
Sunday

Reel
______

M ________________

T ________________

W ________________

T ________________

F ________________

S ________________

S ________________

On Twitter, you want to talk with your audience, not at your audience.

Dates: ______________________________

Board Name T/F

Add your title

Describe your pin

Your website

Board Name S

Add your title

Describe your pin

Your website

Mon

Tweet about your company

Tues

Tweet about a product/service

Wed

Tweet highlighting one of your online reviews

Thurs

Tweet about your industry

Fri

Tweet about something trending this week

Sat

Tweet about an upcoming sale or season

Sun

Tweet an answer to an FAQ in your industry

Weekly Hashtags ______________________________

Industry News ______________________________

Weekly Winners: MOST COMMENTS: LIKES: SHARES: ______________________________

Board Name S/M

Add your title

Describe your pin

Your website

Board Name T/W

Add your title

Describe your pin

Your website

Your Account
Monday
Post about a your company

Your Account
Tuesday
Post about a product/service

Your Account
Wednesday
Post about your industry

Ideas:

Your Account
Sunday
Post a link to a blog or person you respect & your opinion

Your Account
Thursday
Post about your staff

Your Account
Friday
Post about your business logo & info

Your Account
Saturday
Post your opinion on a trending topic

Ideas:

Business Picture
Monday

Behind the scenes clip
Tuesday

Branding Visual
Wednesday

Product/Service
Thursday

Industry Trivia/Fact
Friday

Featured Review
Saturday

Industry FAQ
Sunday

Reel

M ____

T ____

W ____

T ____

F ____

S ____

S ____

Over 200 billion pins have been placed.

Dates: ____________________

Board Name T/F

Add your title

Describe your pin

Your website

Board Name S

Add your title

Describe your pin

Your website

Mon

Tweet about your company

Tues

Tweet about a product/service

Wed

Tweet highlighting one of your online reviews

Thurs

Tweet about your industry

Fri

Tweet about something trending this week

Sat

Tweet about an upcoming sale or season

Sun

Tweet an answer to an FAQ in your industry

Weekly Hashtags ____________________

Industry News ____________________

Weekly Winners: MOST COMMENTS: LIKES: SHARES:

Board Name S/M

Add your title

Describe your pin

Your website

Board Name T/W

Add your title

Describe your pin

Your website

Your Account
Monday
Post about a your company

Your Account
Tuesday
Post about a product/service

Your Account
Wednesday
Post about your industry

Ideas:

Your Account
Sunday
Post a link to a blog or person you respect & your opinion

Your Account
Thursday
Post about your staff

Your Account
Friday
Post about your business logo & info

Your Account
Saturday
Post your opinion on a trending topic

Ideas:

Business Picture
Monday

Behind the scenes clip
Tuesday

Branding Visual
Wednesday

Product/Service
Thursday

Industry Trivia/Fact
Friday

Featured Review
Saturday

Industry FAQ
Sunday

Reel

M ______________________________

T ______________________________

W ______________________________

T ______________________________

F ______________________________

S ______________________________

S ______________________________

____

____

____

____

TikTok has 100 million monthly active users.

Dates: ______________________________

Board Name T/F

Add your title

Describe your pin

Your website

Board Name S

Add your title

Describe your pin

Your website

Mon

- Tweet about your company

Tues

- Tweet about a product/service

Wed

- Tweet highlighting one of your online reviews

Thurs

- Tweet about your industry

Fri

- Tweet about something trending this week

Sat

- Tweet about an upcoming sale or season

Sun

- Tweet an answer to an FAQ in your industry

Weekly Hashtags ______________________________

Industry News ______________________________

Weekly Winners: MOST COMMENTS: LIKES: SHARES:

Board Name S/M

Add your title

Describe your pin

Your website

Board Name T/W

Add your title

Describe your pin

Your website

Your Account
Monday
Post about a your company

Your Account
Tuesday
Post about a product/service

Your Account
Wednesday
Post about your industry

Ideas:

Your Account
Sunday
Post a link to a blog or person you respect & your opinion

Your Account
Thursday
Post about your staff

Your Account
Friday
Post about your business logo & info

Your Account
Saturday
Post your opinion on a trending topic

Ideas:

Business Picture
Monday

Behind the scenes clip
Tuesday

Branding Visual
Wednesday

Product/Service
Thursday

Industry Trivia/Fact
Friday

Featured Review
Saturday

Industry FAQ
Sunday

Reel
______

M ____________________

T ____________________

W ____________________

T ____________________

F ____________________

S ____________________

S ____________________

The average Snapchat user spends 30 minutes on the app per day. Say something quick!

Dates: ____________________

Board Name T/F

Add your title

Describe your pin

Your website

Board Name S

Add your title

Describe your pin

Your website

Mon

Tweet about your company

Tues

Tweet about a product/service

Wed

Tweet highlighting one of your online reviews

Thurs

Tweet about your industry

Fri

Tweet about something trending this week

Sat

Tweet about an upcoming sale or season

Sun

Tweet an answer to an FAQ in your industry

Weekly Hashtags ____________________

Industry News ____________________

Weekly Winners: MOST COMMENTS: LIKES: SHARES:

Board Name S/M

Add your title

Describe your pin

Your website

Board Name T/W

Add your title

Describe your pin

Your website

Your Account
Monday
Post about a your company

Your Account
Tuesday
Post about a product/service

Your Account
Wednesday
Post about your industry

Ideas:

Your Account
Sunday
Post a link to a blog or person you respect & your opinion

Your Account
Thursday
Post about your staff

Your Account
Friday
Post about your business logo & info

Your Account
Saturday
Post your opinion on a trending topic

Ideas:

Business Picture
Monday

Behind the scenes clip
Tuesday

Branding Visual
Wednesday

Product/Service
Thursday

Industry Trivia/Fact
Friday

Featured Review
Saturday

Industry FAQ
Sunday

Reel
______

M ____________________

T ____________________

W ____________________

T ____________________

F ____________________

S ____________________

S ____________________

You can use Twitter to get real-time consumer feedback as well as gauge sentiment regarding products and services.

Dates: ____________________

Board Name T/F

Add your title

Describe your pin

Your website

Board Name S

Add your title

Describe your pin

Your website

Mon

Tweet about your company

Tues

Tweet about a product/service

Wed

Tweet highlighting one of your online reviews

Thurs

Tweet about your industry

Fri

Tweet about something trending this week

Sat

Tweet about an upcoming sale or season

Sun

Tweet an answer to an FAQ in your industry

Weekly Hashtags ____________________

Industry News ____________________

Weekly Winners: MOST COMMENTS: LIKES: SHARES: ____________________

Board Name S/M

Add your title

Describe your pin

Your website

Board Name T/W

Add your title

Describe your pin

Your website

Your Account
Monday
Post about a your company

Your Account
Tuesday
Post about a product/service

Your Account
Wednesday
Post about your industry

Ideas:

Your Account
Sunday
Post a link to a blog or person you respect & your opinion

Your Account
Thursday
Post about your staff

Your Account
Friday
Post about your business logo & info

Your Account
Saturday
Post your opinion on a trending topic

Ideas:

Business Picture
Monday

Behind the scenes clip
Tuesday

Branding Visual
Wednesday

Product/Service
Thursday

Industry Trivia/Fact
Friday

Featured Review
Saturday

Industry FAQ
Sunday

Reel
______

M ______________________

T ______________________

W ______________________

T ______________________

F ______________________

S ______________________

S ______________________

____

____

____

____

1.8 billion of Facebook users (66%) use the app on a daily basis.
Even if you don't like Facebook, post there.

Dates: ______________________________

Board Name T/F

Add your title

Describe your pin

Your website

Board Name S

Add your title

Describe your pin

Your website

Mon

Tweet about your company

Tues

Tweet about a product/service

Wed

Tweet highlighting one of your online reviews

Thurs

Tweet about your industry

Fri

Tweet about something trending this week

Sat

Tweet about an upcoming sale or season

Sun

Tweet an answer to an FAQ in your industry

Weekly Hashtags ______________________________

Industry News ______________________________

Weekly Winners: MOST COMMENTS: LIKES: SHARES:

Board Name S/M

Add your title

Describe your pin

Your website

Board Name T/W

Add your title

Describe your pin

Your website

Your Account
Monday
Post about a your company

Your Account
Tuesday
Post about a product/service

Your Account
Wednesday
Post about your industry

Ideas:

Your Account
Sunday
Post a link to a blog or person you respect & your opinion

Your Account
Thursday
Post about your staff

Your Account
Friday
Post about your business logo & info

Your Account
Saturday
Post your opinion on a trending topic

Ideas:

Business Picture
Monday

Behind the scenes clip
Tuesday

Branding Visual
Wednesday

Product/Service
Thursday

Industry Trivia/Fact
Friday

Featured Review
Saturday

Industry FAQ
Sunday

Reel
______

M ____________________

T ____________________

W ____________________

T ____________________

F ____________________

S ____________________

S ____________________

____

____

____

____

The largest demographic on Pinterest is 35-49 years old. What's something from your business you would pin?

Dates: ____________________

Board Name T/F

Add your title

Describe your pin

Your website

Board Name S

Add your title

Describe your pin

Your website

Mon

Tweet about your company

Tues

Tweet about a product/service

Wed

Tweet highlighting one of your online reviews

Thurs

Tweet about your industry

Fri

Tweet about something trending this week

Sat

Tweet about an upcoming sale or season

Sun

Tweet an answer to an FAQ in your industry

Weekly Hashtags ____________________

Industry News ____________________

Weekly Winners: MOST COMMENTS: LIKES: SHARES: ____________________

Board Name S/M

Add your title

Describe your pin

Your website

Board Name T/W

Add your title

Describe your pin

Your website

Your Account
Monday
Post about a your company

Your Account
Tuesday
Post about a product/service

Your Account
Wednesday
Post about your industry

Ideas:

Your Account
Sunday
Post a link to a blog or person you respect & your opinion

Your Account
Thursday
Post about your staff

Your Account
Friday
Post about your business logo & info

Your Account
Saturday
Post your opinion on a trending topic

Ideas:

Business Picture
Monday

Behind the scenes clip
Tuesday

Branding Visual
Wednesday

Product/Service
Thursday

Industry Trivia/Fact
Friday

Featured Review
Saturday

Industry FAQ
Sunday

Reel
______

M ______________________

T ______________________

W ______________________

T ______________________

F ______________________

S ______________________

S ______________________

____

____

____

____

April 2012, instagram was sold to Facebook for $1 billion.

Dates: ______

Board Name T/F

Add your title

Describe your pin

Your website

Board Name S

Add your title

Describe your pin

Your website

Mon

Tweet about your company

Tues

Tweet about a product/service

Wed

Tweet highlighting one of your online reviews

Thurs

Tweet about your industry

Fri

Tweet about something trending this week

Sat

Tweet about an upcoming sale or season

Sun

Tweet an answer to an FAQ in your industry

Weekly Hashtags ______

Industry News ______

Weekly Winners: MOST COMMENTS: LIKES: SHARES:

Board Name S/M

Add your title

Describe your pin

Your website

Board Name T/W

Add your title

Describe your pin

Your website

Your Account
Monday
Post about a your company

Your Account
Tuesday
Post about a product/service

Your Account
Wednesday
Post about your industry

Ideas:

Your Account
Sunday
Post a link to a blog or person you respect & your opinion

Your Account
Thursday
Post about your staff

Your Account
Friday
Post about your business logo & info

Your Account
Saturday
Post your opinion on a trending topic

Ideas:

Business Picture
Monday

Behind the scenes clip
Tuesday

Branding Visual
Wednesday

Product/Service
Thursday

Industry Trivia/Fact
Friday

Featured Review
Saturday

Industry FAQ
Sunday

Reel
______

M ____________________

T ____________________

W ____________________

T ____________________

F ____________________

S ____________________

S ____________________

In 2019, users opened Snapchat 30 times a day on average.

Dates: ______________________________

Board Name T/F

Add your title

Describe your pin

Your website

Board Name S

Add your title

Describe your pin

Your website

Mon

Tweet about your company

Tues

Tweet about a product/service

Wed

Tweet highlighting one of your online reviews

Thurs

Tweet about your industry

Fri

Tweet about something trending this week

Sat

Tweet about an upcoming sale or season

Sun

Tweet an answer to an FAQ in your industry

Weekly Hashtags ______________________________

Industry News ______________________________

Weekly Winners: MOST COMMENTS: LIKES: SHARES:

Board Name S/M

Add your title

Describe your pin

Your website

Board Name T/W

Add your title

Describe your pin

Your website

Your Account
Monday
Post about a your company

Your Account
Tuesday
Post about a product/service

Your Account
Wednesday
Post about your industry

Ideas:

Your Account
Sunday
Post a link to a blog or person you respect & your opinion

Your Account
Thursday
Post about your staff

Your Account
Friday
Post about your business logo & info

Your Account
Saturday
Post your opinion on a trending topic

Ideas:

Business Picture
Monday

Behind the scenes clip
Tuesday

Branding Visual
Wednesday

Product/Service
Thursday

Industry Trivia/Fact
Friday

Featured Review
Saturday

Industry FAQ
Sunday

Reel
______

M ______________________

T ______________________

W ______________________

T ______________________

F ______________________

S ______________________

S ______________________

There are 500 million daily active users of Instagram Stories.

Dates: ______________________________

Board Name T/F

Add your title

Describe your pin

Your website

Board Name S

Add your title

Describe your pin

Your website

Mon

- Tweet about your company

Tues

- Tweet about a product/service

Wed

- Tweet highlighting one of your online reviews

Thurs

- Tweet about your industry

Fri

- Tweet about something trending this week

Sat

- Tweet about an upcoming sale or season

Sun

- Tweet an answer to an FAQ in your industry

Weekly Hashtags ______________________________

Industry News ______________________________

Weekly Winners: MOST COMMENTS: LIKES: SHARES:

Board Name S/M

Add your title

Describe your pin

Your website

Board Name T/W

Add your title

Describe your pin

Your website

Your Account
Monday
Post about a your company

Your Account
Tuesday
Post about a product/service

Your Account
Wednesday
Post about your industry

Ideas:

Your Account
Sunday
Post a link to a blog or person you respect & your opinion

Your Account
Thursday
Post about your staff

Your Account
Friday
Post about your business logo & info

Your Account
Saturday
Post your opinion on a trending topic

Ideas:

Business Picture
Monday

Behind the scenes clip
Tuesday

Branding Visual
Wednesday

Product/Service
Thursday

Industry Trivia/Fact
Friday

Featured Review
Saturday

Industry FAQ
Sunday

Reel
______

M ____________________

T ____________________

W ____________________

T ____________________

F ____________________

S ____________________

S ____________________

57 percent of Pinterest users access the platform once a week.

Dates: ______________________________

Board Name T/F

Add your title

Describe your pin

Your website

Board Name S

Add your title

Describe your pin

Your website

Mon

Tweet about your company

Tues

Tweet about a product/service

Wed

Tweet highlighting one of your online reviews

Thurs

Tweet about your industry

Fri

Tweet about something trending this week

Sat

Tweet about an upcoming sale or season

Sun

Tweet an answer to an FAQ in your industry

Weekly Hashtags ______________________________

Industry News ______________________________

Weekly Winners: MOST COMMENTS: LIKES: SHARES:

Board Name S/M

Add your title

Describe your pin

Your website

Board Name T/W

Add your title

Describe your pin

Your website

Your Account
Monday
Post about a your company

Your Account
Tuesday
Post about a product/service

Your Account
Wednesday
Post about your industry

Ideas:

Your Account
Sunday
Post a link to a blog or person you respect & your opinion

Your Account
Thursday
Post about your staff

Your Account
Friday
Post about your business logo & info

Your Account
Saturday
Post your opinion on a trending topic

Ideas:

Business Picture
Monday

Behind the scenes clip
Tuesday

Branding Visual
Wednesday

Product/Service
Thursday

Industry Trivia/Fact
Friday

Featured Review
Saturday

Industry FAQ
Sunday

Reel

M

T

W

T

F

S

S

TikTok is attracting older users rapidly, so don't be discouraged to have a presence on TikTok, even if your target audience isn't a young demographic.

Dates: ______________________________

Board Name T/F

Add your title

Describe your pin

Your website

Board Name S

Add your title

Describe your pin

Your website

Mon

Tweet about your company

Tues

Tweet about a product/service

Wed

Tweet highlighting one of your online reviews

Thurs

Tweet about your industry

Fri

Tweet about something trending this week

Sat

Tweet about an upcoming sale or season

Sun

Tweet an answer to an FAQ in your industry

Weekly Hashtags ______________________________

Industry News ______________________________

Weekly Winners: MOST COMMENTS: LIKES: SHARES:

Board Name S/M

Add your title

Describe your pin

Your website

Board Name T/W

Add your title

Describe your pin

Your website

Your Account
Monday
Post about a your company

Your Account
Tuesday
Post about a product/service

Your Account
Wednesday
Post about your industry

Ideas:

Your Account
Sunday
Post a link to a blog or person you respect & your opinion

Your Account
Thursday
Post about your staff

Your Account
Friday
Post about your business logo & info

Your Account
Saturday
Post your opinion on a trending topic

Ideas:

Business Picture
Monday

Behind the scenes clip
Tuesday

Branding Visual
Wednesday

Product/Service
Thursday

Industry Trivia/Fact
Friday

Featured Review
Saturday

Industry FAQ
Sunday

Reel
______

M ____________________

T ____________________

W ____________________

T ____________________

F ____________________

S ____________________

S ____________________

____

____

____

____

Although 46% of the US adult population is over 50, only 15% of images containing adults include people in that age segment, according to a study done by AARP, so make sure you include images of your target market, so everyone can be represented.

Dates: ______________________________

Board Name T/F

Add your title

Describe your pin

Your website

Board Name S

Add your title

Describe your pin

Your website

Mon

Tweet about your company

Tues

Tweet about a product/service

Wed

Tweet highlighting one of your online reviews

Thurs

Tweet about your industry

Fri

Tweet about something trending this week

Sat

Tweet about an upcoming sale or season

Sun

Tweet an answer to an FAQ in your industry

Weekly Hashtags ______________________________

Industry News ______________________________

Weekly Winners: MOST COMMENTS: LIKES: SHARES:

Board Name S/M

Add your title

Describe your pin

Your website

Board Name T/W

Add your title

Describe your pin

Your website

Your Account
Monday
Post about a your company

Your Account
Tuesday
Post about a product/service

Your Account
Wednesday
Post about your industry

Ideas:

Your Account
Sunday
Post a link to a blog or person you respect & your opinion

Your Account
Thursday
Post about your staff

Your Account
Friday
Post about your business logo & info

Your Account
Saturday
Post your opinion on a trending topic

Ideas:

Business Picture
Monday

Behind the scenes clip
Tuesday

Branding Visual
Wednesday

Product/Service
Thursday

Industry Trivia/Fact
Friday

Featured Review
Saturday

Industry FAQ
Sunday

Reel

M ____________________

T ____________________

W ____________________

T ____________________

F ____________________

S ____________________

S ____________________

70% of users 55-64 say they've bought something online in the past month. Make sure they can find your products through social media.

Dates: ______________________________

Board Name T/F

Add your title

Describe your pin

Your website

Board Name S

Add your title

Describe your pin

Your website

Mon

Tweet about your company

Tues

Tweet about a product/service

Wed

Tweet highlighting one of your online reviews

Thurs

Tweet about your industry

Fri

Tweet about something trending this week

Sat

Tweet about an upcoming sale or season

Sun

Tweet an answer to an FAQ in your industry

Weekly Hashtags ______________________________

Industry News ______________________________

Weekly Winners: MOST COMMENTS: LIKES: SHARES:

Board Name S/M

Add your title

Describe your pin

Your website

Board Name T/W

Add your title

Describe your pin

Your website

Your Account
Monday
Post about a your company

Your Account
Tuesday
Post about a product/service

Your Account
Wednesday
Post about your industry

Ideas:

Your Account
Sunday
Post a link to a blog or person you respect & your opinion

Your Account
Thursday
Post about your staff

Your Account
Friday
Post about your business logo & info

Your Account
Saturday
Post your opinion on a trending topic

Ideas:

Business Picture
Monday

Behind the scenes clip
Tuesday

Branding Visual
Wednesday

Product/Service
Thursday

Industry Trivia/Fact
Friday

Featured Review
Saturday

Industry FAQ
Sunday

Reel
______

M ____________________

T ____________________

W ____________________

T ____________________

F ____________________

S ____________________

S ____________________

Twitter is the 11th most visited site in the world because you don't need an account to read Tweets. Even if you're not getting retweets and replies, people are finding your content.

Dates: ______________________________

Board Name T/F

Add your title

Describe your pin

Your website

Board Name S

Add your title

Describe your pin

Your website

Mon

Tweet about your company

Tues

Tweet about a product/service

Wed

Tweet highlighting one of your online reviews

Thurs

Tweet about your industry

Fri

Tweet about something trending this week

Sat

Tweet about an upcoming sale or season

Sun

Tweet an answer to an FAQ in your industry

Weekly Hashtags ______________________________

Industry News ______________________________

Weekly Winners: MOST COMMENTS: LIKES: SHARES:

Board Name S/M

Add your title

Describe your pin

Your website

Board Name T/W

Add your title

Describe your pin

Your website

Your Account
Monday
Post about a your company

Your Account
Tuesday
Post about a product/service

Your Account
Wednesday
Post about your industry

Ideas:

Your Account
Sunday
Post a link to a blog or person you respect & your opinion

Your Account
Thursday
Post about your staff

Your Account
Friday
Post about your business logo & info

Your Account
Saturday
Post your opinion on a trending topic

Ideas:

Business Picture
Monday

Behind the scenes clip
Tuesday

Branding Visual
Wednesday

Product/Service
Thursday

Industry Trivia/Fact
Friday

Featured Review
Saturday

Industry FAQ
Sunday

Reel
______

M ______

T ______

W ______

T ______

F ______

S ______

S ______

Video creation on TikTok is a conversation, so ask a question and you'll be able to see replies from users in the comments or through videos of their own based on yours.

Dates: ________________________________

Board Name T/F

Add your title

Describe your pin

Your website

Board Name S

Add your title

Describe your pin

Your website

Mon

Tweet about your company

Thurs

Tweet about your industry

Tues

Tweet about a product/service

Fri

Tweet about something trending this week

Sat

Tweet about an upcoming sale or season

Wed

Tweet highlighting one of your online reviews

Sun

Tweet an answer to an FAQ in your industry

Weekly Hashtags ________________________________

Industry News ________________________________

Weekly Winners: MOST COMMENTS: LIKES: SHARES: ________________________________

Board Name S/M

Add your title

Describe your pin

Your website

Board Name T/W

Add your title

Describe your pin

Your website

Your Account
Monday
Post about a your company

Your Account
Tuesday
Post about a product/service

Your Account
Wednesday
Post about your industry

Ideas:

Your Account
Sunday
Post a link to a blog or person you respect & your opinion

Your Account
Thursday
Post about your staff

Your Account
Friday
Post about your business logo & info

Your Account
Saturday
Post your opinion on a trending topic

Ideas:

Business Picture
Monday

Behind the scenes clip
Tuesday

Branding Visual
Wednesday

Product/Service
Thursday

Industry Trivia/Fact
Friday

Featured Review
Saturday

Industry FAQ
Sunday

Reel

M ______________________

T ______________________

W ______________________

T ______________________

F ______________________

S ______________________

S ______________________

Only a small minority of online users actually comment or share content—the vast majority of all online media is consumed passively, so don't be discouraged. keep posting!

Dates: ____________________

Board Name T/F

Add your title

Describe your pin

Your website

Board Name S

Add your title

Describe your pin

Your website

Mon

Tweet about your company

Tues

Tweet about a product/service

Wed

Tweet highlighting one of your online reviews

Thurs

Tweet about your industry

Fri

Tweet about something trending this week

Sat

Tweet about an upcoming sale or season

Sun

Tweet an answer to an FAQ in your industry

Weekly Hashtags ____________________

Industry News ____________________

Weekly Winners: MOST COMMENTS: LIKES: SHARES:

Board Name S/M

Add your title

Describe your pin

Your website

Board Name T/W

Add your title

Describe your pin

Your website

Your Account
Monday
Post about a your company

Your Account
Tuesday
Post about a product/service

Your Account
Wednesday
Post about your industry

Ideas:

Your Account
Sunday
Post a link to a blog or person you respect & your opinion

Your Account
Thursday
Post about your staff

Your Account
Friday
Post about your business logo & info

Your Account
Saturday
Post your opinion on a trending topic

Ideas:

Business Picture
Monday

Behind the scenes clip
Tuesday

Branding Visual
Wednesday

Product/Service
Thursday

Industry Trivia/Fact
Friday

Featured Review
Saturday

Industry FAQ
Sunday

Reel

M ____________________

T ____________________

W ____________________

T ____________________

F ____________________

S ____________________

S ____________________

Every pin on Pintrest has to have a source link (likely your website URL), so people who see your pins can be taken to your website if they're interested in what you're posting.

Dates: ______________________________

Board Name T/F

Add your title

Describe your pin

Your website

Board Name S

Add your title

Describe your pin

Your website

Mon

Tweet about your company

Tues

Tweet about a product/service

Wed

Tweet highlighting one of your online reviews

Thurs

Tweet about your industry

Fri

Tweet about something trending this week

Sat

Tweet about an upcoming sale or season

Sun

Tweet an answer to an FAQ in your industry

Weekly Hashtags ______________________________

Industry News ______________________________

Weekly Winners: MOST COMMENTS: LIKES: SHARES: ______________________________

Board Name S/M

Add your title

Describe your pin

Your website

Board Name T/W

Add your title

Describe your pin

Your website

Your Account
Monday
Post about a your company

Your Account
Tuesday
Post about a product/service

Your Account
Wednesday
Post about your industry

Ideas:

Your Account
Sunday
Post a link to a blog or person you respect & your opinion

Your Account
Thursday
Post about your staff

Your Account
Friday
Post about your business logo & info

Your Account
Saturday
Post your opinion on a trending topic

Ideas:

Business Picture
Monday

Behind the scenes clip
Tuesday

Branding Visual
Wednesday

Product/Service
Thursday

Industry Trivia/Fact
Friday

Featured Review
Saturday

Industry FAQ
Sunday

Reel

M ______

T ______

W ______

T ______

F ______

S ______

S ______

When you record a TikTok video, you get video editing options on the screen that make it easy to add songs in the background, animations, graphics, and text to your videos.

Dates: ____________________

Board Name T/F

Add your title

Describe your pin

Your website

Board Name S

Add your title

Describe your pin

Your website

Mon

Tweet about your company

Tues

Tweet about a product/service

Wed

Tweet highlighting one of your online reviews

Thurs

Tweet about your industry

Fri

Tweet about something trending this week

Sat

Tweet about an upcoming sale or season

Sun

Tweet an answer to an FAQ in your industry

Weekly Hashtags ____________________

Industry News ____________________

Weekly Winners: MOST COMMENTS: LIKES: SHARES: ____________________

Board Name S/M

Add your title

Describe your pin

Your website

Board Name T/W

Add your title

Describe your pin

Your website

Your Account
Monday
Post about a your company

Your Account
Tuesday
Post about a product/service

Your Account
Wednesday
Post about your industry

Ideas:

Your Account
Sunday
Post a link to a blog or person you respect & your opinion

Your Account
Thursday
Post about your staff

Your Account
Friday
Post about your business logo & info

Your Account
Saturday
Post your opinion on a trending topic

Ideas:

Business Picture
Monday

Behind the scenes clip
Tuesday

Branding Visual
Wednesday

Product/Service
Thursday

Industry Trivia/Fact
Friday

Featured Review
Saturday

Industry FAQ
Sunday

Reel
______

M ____________________

T ____________________

W ____________________

T ____________________

F ____________________

S ____________________

S ____________________

____

____

____

____

TikTok's easy-to-use augmented reality, video editing and music features allow people to explore their creative side in a simple way.

Dates: ____________________

Board Name T/F

Add your title

Describe your pin

Your website

Board Name S

Add your title

Describe your pin

Your website

Mon

Tweet about your company

Tues

Tweet about a product/service

Wed

Tweet highlighting one of your online reviews

Thurs

Tweet about your industry

Fri

Tweet about something trending this week

Sat

Tweet about an upcoming sale or season

Sun

Tweet an answer to an FAQ in your industry

Weekly Hashtags ____________________

Industry News ____________________

Weekly Winners: MOST COMMENTS: LIKES: SHARES: ____________________

Board Name S/M

Add your title

Describe your pin

Your website

Board Name T/W

Add your title

Describe your pin

Your website

Your Account
Monday
Post about a your company

Your Account
Tuesday
Post about a product/service

Your Account
Wednesday
Post about your industry

Ideas:

Your Account
Sunday
Post a link to a blog or person you respect & your opinion

Your Account
Thursday
Post about your staff

Your Account
Friday
Post about your business logo & info

Your Account
Saturday
Post your opinion on a trending topic

Ideas:

Business Picture
Monday

Behind the scenes clip
Tuesday

Branding Visual
Wednesday

Product/Service
Thursday

Industry Trivia/Fact
Friday

Featured Review
Saturday

Industry FAQ
Sunday

Reel
______

M ______________________

T ______________________

W ______________________

T ______________________

F ______________________

S ______________________

S ______________________

More than half of businesses (60%) are planning to increase their Instagram budget.

Dates: ______________________________

Board Name T/F

Add your title

Describe your pin

Your website

Board Name S

Add your title

Describe your pin

Your website

Mon

Tweet about your company

Tues

Tweet about a product/service

Wed

Tweet highlighting one of your online reviews

Thurs

Tweet about your industry

Fri

Tweet about something trending this week

Sat

Tweet about an upcoming sale or season

Sun

Tweet an answer to an FAQ in your industry

Weekly Hashtags ______________________________

Industry News ______________________________

Weekly Winners: MOST COMMENTS: LIKES: SHARES:

Board Name S/M

Add your title

Describe your pin

Your website

Board Name T/W

Add your title

Describe your pin

Your website

Your Account
Monday
Post about a your company

Your Account
Tuesday
Post about a product/service

Your Account
Wednesday
Post about your industry

Ideas:

Your Account
Sunday
Post a link to a blog or person you respect & your opinion

Your Account
Thursday
Post about your staff

Your Account
Friday
Post about your business logo & info

Your Account
Saturday
Post your opinion on a trending topic

Ideas:

Business Picture
Monday

Behind the scenes clip
Tuesday

Branding Visual
Wednesday

Product/Service
Thursday

Industry Trivia/Fact
Friday

Featured Review
Saturday

Industry FAQ
Sunday

Reel
______

M ______________________

T ______________________

W ______________________

T ______________________

F ______________________

S ______________________

S ______________________

____

____

____

____

78% of businesses consider Facebook the most effective platform for reaching business goals.

Dates: ______________________________

Board Name **T/F**

Add your title

Describe your pin

Your website

Board Name **S**

Add your title

Describe your pin

Your website

Mon

- Tweet about your company

Tues

- Tweet about a product/service

Wed

- Tweet highlighting one of your online reviews

Thurs

- Tweet about your industry

Fri

- Tweet about something trending this week

Sat

- Tweet about an upcoming sale or season

Sun

- Tweet an answer to an FAQ in your industry

Weekly Hashtags ______________________________

Industry News ______________________________

Weekly Winners: MOST COMMENTS: LIKES: SHARES:

Board Name S/M

Add your title

Describe your pin

Your website

Board Name T/W

Add your title

Describe your pin

Your website

Your Account
Monday
Post about a your company

Your Account
Tuesday
Post about a product/service

Your Account
Wednesday
Post about your industry

Ideas:

Your Account
Sunday
Post a link to a blog or person you respect & your opinion

Your Account
Thursday
Post about your staff

Your Account
Friday
Post about your business logo & info

Your Account
Saturday
Post your opinion on a trending topic

Ideas:

Business Picture
Monday

Behind the scenes clip
Tuesday

Branding Visual
Wednesday

Product/Service
Thursday

M ______________________

T ______________________

W ______________________

T ______________________

F ______________________

S ______________________

S ______________________

Industry Trivia/Fact
Friday

Featured Review
Saturday

Industry FAQ
Sunday

Reel

While retail remains the dominant use case for Pinterest, 2021 saw rising use of Pinterest among brands in the education, advertising, and business and professional services industries.

Dates: ______________________________

Board Name T/F

Add your title

Describe your pin

Your website

Board Name S

Add your title

Describe your pin

Your website

Mon

Tweet about your company

Tues

Tweet about a product/service

Wed

Tweet highlighting one of your online reviews

Thurs

Tweet about your industry

Fri

Tweet about something trending this week

Sat

Tweet about an upcoming sale or season

Sun

Tweet an answer to an FAQ in your industry

Weekly Hashtags ______________________________

Industry News ______________________________

Weekly Winners: MOST COMMENTS: LIKES: SHARES:

Board Name S/M

Add your title

Describe your pin

Your website

Board Name T/W

Add your title

Describe your pin

Your website

Your Account
Monday
Post about a your company

Your Account
Tuesday
Post about a product/service

Your Account
Wednesday
Post about your industry

Ideas:

Your Account
Sunday
Post a link to a blog or person you respect & your opinion

Your Account
Thursday
Post about your staff

Your Account
Friday
Post about your business logo & info

Your Account
Saturday
Post your opinion on a trending topic

Ideas:

Business Picture
Monday

Behind the scenes clip
Tuesday

Branding Visual
Wednesday

Product/Service
Thursday

Industry Trivia/Fact
Friday

Featured Review
Saturday

Industry FAQ
Sunday

Reel
______

M ____________________

T ____________________

W ____________________

T ____________________

F ____________________

S ____________________

S ____________________

If you don't like your voice, no problem! TikTok not only encourages voice-over, but offers a range of effects, so you can have a narrator on your video.

Dates: ______________________________

Board Name T/F

Add your title

Describe your pin

Your website

Board Name S

Add your title

Describe your pin

Your website

Mon

Tweet about your company

Tues

Tweet about a product/service

Wed

Tweet highlighting one of your online reviews

Thurs

Tweet about your industry

Fri

Tweet about something trending this week

Sat

Tweet about an upcoming sale or season

Sun

Tweet an answer to an FAQ in your industry

Weekly Hashtags ______________________________

Industry News ______________________________

Weekly Winners: MOST COMMENTS: LIKES: SHARES: ______________________________

Board Name S/M

Add your title

Describe your pin

Your website

Board Name T/W

Add your title

Describe your pin

Your website

Your Account
Monday
Post about a your company

Your Account
Tuesday
Post about a product/service

Your Account
Wednesday
Post about your industry

Ideas:

Your Account
Sunday
Post a link to a blog or person you respect & your opinion

Your Account
Thursday
Post about your staff

Your Account
Friday
Post about your business logo & info

Your Account
Saturday
Post your opinion on a trending topic

Ideas:

Business Picture
Monday

Behind the scenes clip
Tuesday

Branding Visual
Wednesday

Product/Service
Thursday

Industry Trivia/Fact
Friday

Featured Review
Saturday

Industry FAQ
Sunday

Reel

M ______________________

T ______________________

W ______________________

T ______________________

F ______________________

S ______________________

S ______________________

Pinterest has a "visual search" feature that lets users identify, and sometimes even buy products in a pin.

Dates: ______________________________

Board Name T/F

Add your title

Describe your pin

Your website

Board Name S

Add your title

Describe your pin

Your website

Mon

Tweet about your company

Tues

Tweet about a product/service

Wed

Tweet highlighting one of your online reviews

Thurs

Tweet about your industry

Fri

Tweet about something trending this week

Sat

Tweet about an upcoming sale or season

Sun

Tweet an answer to an FAQ in your industry

Weekly Hashtags ______________________________

Industry News ______________________________

Weekly Winners: MOST COMMENTS: LIKES: SHARES: ______________________________

Board Name S/M

Add your title

Describe your pin

Your website

Board Name T/W

Add your title

Describe your pin

Your website

Your Account
Monday
Post about a your company

Your Account
Tuesday
Post about a product/service

Your Account
Wednesday
Post about your industry

Ideas:

Your Account
Sunday
Post a link to a blog or person you respect & your opinion

Your Account
Thursday
Post about your staff

Your Account
Friday
Post about your business logo & info

Your Account
Saturday
Post your opinion on a trending topic

Ideas:

Business Picture
Monday

Behind the scenes clip
Tuesday

Branding Visual
Wednesday

Product/Service
Thursday

Industry Trivia/Fact
Friday

Featured Review
Saturday

Industry FAQ
Sunday

Reel

M ______________________

T ______________________

W ______________________

T ______________________

F ______________________

S ______________________

S ______________________

Tik Tok is a sound-dominant platform. Just by changing the sound, you can drastically improve performance

Dates: ______________________________

Board Name T/F

Add your title

Describe your pin

Your website

Board Name S

Add your title

Describe your pin

Your website

Mon

Tweet about your company

Tues

Tweet about a product/service

Wed

Tweet highlighting one of your online reviews

Thurs

Tweet about your industry

Fri

Tweet about something trending this week

Sat

Tweet about an upcoming sale or season

Sun

Tweet an answer to an FAQ in your industry

Weekly Hashtags ______________________________

Industry News ______________________________

Weekly Winners: MOST COMMENTS: LIKES: SHARES:

Board Name S/M

Add your title

Describe your pin

Your website

Board Name T/W

Add your title

Describe your pin

Your website

Your Account
Monday
Post about a your company

Your Account
Tuesday
Post about a product/service

Your Account
Wednesday
Post about your industry

Ideas:

Your Account
Sunday
Post a link to a blog or person you respect & your opinion

Your Account
Thursday
Post about your staff

Your Account
Friday
Post about your business logo & info

Your Account
Saturday
Post your opinion on a trending topic

Ideas:

Business Picture
Monday

Behind the scenes clip
Tuesday

Branding Visual
Wednesday

Product/Service
Thursday

Industry Trivia/Fact
Friday

Featured Review
Saturday

Industry FAQ
Sunday

Reel

M ____________________

T ____________________

W ____________________

T ____________________

F ____________________

S ____________________

S ____________________

70% of people feel that brands online should be positive while also being mindful of the cultural environment, so share an opinion about the about the cultural context in which we live!

Dates: ____________________

Board Name T/F

Add your title

Describe your pin

Your website

Board Name S

Add your title

Describe your pin

Your website

Mon

Tweet about your company

Tues

Tweet about a product/service

Wed

Tweet highlighting one of your online reviews

Thurs

Tweet about your industry

Fri

Tweet about something trending this week

Sat

Tweet about an upcoming sale or season

Sun

Tweet an answer to an FAQ in your industry

Weekly Hashtags ____________________

Industry News ____________________

Weekly Winners: MOST COMMENTS: LIKES: SHARES:

Board Name S/M

Add your title

Describe your pin

Your website

Board Name T/W

Add your title

Describe your pin

Your website

Your Account
Monday
Post about a your company

Your Account
Tuesday
Post about a product/service

Your Account
Wednesday
Post about your industry

Ideas:

Your Account
Sunday
Post a link to a blog or person you respect & your opinion

Your Account
Thursday
Post about your staff

Your Account
Friday
Post about your business logo & info

Your Account
Saturday
Post your opinion on a trending topic

Ideas:

Business Picture
Monday

Behind the scenes clip
Tuesday

Branding Visual
Wednesday

Product/Service
Thursday

Industry Trivia/Fact
Friday

Featured Review
Saturday

Industry FAQ
Sunday

Reel
______

M ____________________

T ____________________

W ____________________

T ____________________

F ____________________

S ____________________

S ____________________

The average Instagram post has 10.7 hashtags, though 50% of posts use fewer than six. Search your competitors and see what hashtags they use.

Dates: ______________________________

Board Name T/F

Add your title

Describe your pin

Your website

Board Name S

Add your title

Describe your pin

Your website

Mon

Tweet about your company

Tues

Tweet about a product/service

Wed

Tweet highlighting one of your online reviews

Thurs

Tweet about your industry

Fri

Tweet about something trending this week

Sat

Tweet about an upcoming sale or season

Sun

Tweet an answer to an FAQ in your industry

Weekly Hashtags ______________________________

Industry News ______________________________

Weekly Winners: MOST COMMENTS: LIKES: SHARES: ______________________________

Board Name S/M

Add your title

Describe your pin

Your website

Board Name T/W

Add your title

Describe your pin

Your website

Your Account
Monday
Post about a your company

Your Account
Tuesday
Post about a product/service

Your Account
Wednesday
Post about your industry

Ideas:

Your Account
Sunday
Post a link to a blog or person you respect & your opinion

Your Account
Thursday
Post about your staff

Your Account
Friday
Post about your business logo & info

Your Account
Saturday
Post your opinion on a trending topic

Ideas:

Business Picture
Monday

Behind the scenes clip
Tuesday

Branding Visual
Wednesday

Product/Service
Thursday

Industry Trivia/Fact
Friday

Featured Review
Saturday

Industry FAQ
Sunday

Reel

M ______

T ______

W ______

T ______

F ______

S ______

S ______

Snapchat usage in the U.S. is projected to increase to 88.5 million users in 2022. That's a lot of opportunities.

Dates: ______________________________

Board Name T/F

Add your title

Describe your pin

Your website

Board Name S

Add your title

Describe your pin

Your website

Mon

Tweet about your company

Tues

Tweet about a product/service

Wed

Tweet highlighting one of your online reviews

Thurs

Tweet about your industry

Fri

Tweet about something trending this week

Sat

Tweet about an upcoming sale or season

Sun

Tweet an answer to an FAQ in your industry

Weekly Hashtags ______________________________

Industry News ______________________________

Weekly Winners: MOST COMMENTS: LIKES: SHARES:

Board Name S/M

Add your title

Describe your pin

Your website

Board Name T/W

Add your title

Describe your pin

Your website

Your Account
Monday
Post about a your company

Your Account
Tuesday
Post about a product/service

Your Account
Wednesday
Post about your industry

Ideas:

Your Account
Sunday
Post a link to a blog or person you respect & your opinion

Your Account
Thursday
Post about your staff

Your Account
Friday
Post about your business logo & info

Your Account
Saturday
Post your opinion on a trending topic

Ideas:

Business Picture
Monday

Behind the scenes clip
Tuesday

Branding Visual
Wednesday

Product/Service
Thursday

Industry Trivia/Fact
Friday

Featured Review
Saturday

Industry FAQ
Sunday

Reel
______

M ____________________

T ____________________

W ____________________

T ____________________

F ____________________

S ____________________

S ____________________

There are 1.16 billion estimated Instagram users worldwide.

Dates: ______________________________

Board Name T/F

Add your title

Describe your pin

Your website

Board Name S

Add your title

Describe your pin

Your website

Mon

Tweet about your company

Tues

Tweet about a product/service

Wed

Tweet highlighting one of your online reviews

Thurs

Tweet about your industry

Fri

Tweet about something trending this week

Sat

Tweet about an upcoming sale or season

Sun

Tweet an answer to an FAQ in your industry

Weekly Hashtags ______________________________

Industry News ______________________________

Weekly Winners: MOST COMMENTS: LIKES: SHARES: ______________________________

Board Name S/M

Add your title

Describe your pin

Your website

Board Name T/W

Add your title

Describe your pin

Your website

Your Account
Monday
Post about a your company

Your Account
Tuesday
Post about a product/service

Your Account
Wednesday
Post about your industry

Ideas:

Your Account
Sunday
Post a link to a blog or person you respect & your opinion

Your Account
Thursday
Post about your staff

Your Account
Friday
Post about your business logo & info

Your Account
Saturday
Post your opinion on a trending topic

Ideas:

Business Picture
Monday

Behind the scenes clip
Tuesday

Branding Visual
Wednesday

Product/Service
Thursday

Industry Trivia/Fact
Friday

Featured Review
Saturday

Industry FAQ
Sunday

Reel

M

T

W

T

F

S

S

When tweeting videos, keep the text of the tweet short. Short text results in 13% higher brand and message recall and overall watch time.

Dates: ____________________

Board Name T/F

Add your title

Describe your pin

Your website

Board Name S

Add your title

Describe your pin

Your website

Mon

Tweet about your company

Tues

Tweet about a product/service

Wed

Tweet highlighting one of your online reviews

Thurs

Tweet about your industry

Fri

Tweet about something trending this week

Sat

Tweet about an upcoming sale or season

Sun

Tweet an answer to an FAQ in your industry

Weekly Hashtags ____________________

Industry News ____________________

Weekly Winners: MOST COMMENTS: LIKES: SHARES:

Board Name S/M

Add your title

Describe your pin

Your website

Board Name T/W

Add your title

Describe your pin

Your website

Your Account
Monday
Post about a your company

Your Account
Tuesday
Post about a product/service

Your Account
Wednesday
Post about your industry

Ideas:

Your Account
Sunday
Post a link to a blog or person you respect & your opinion

Your Account
Thursday
Post about your staff

Your Account
Friday
Post about your business logo & info

Your Account
Saturday
Post your opinion on a trending topic

Ideas:

Business Picture
Monday

Behind the scenes clip
Tuesday

Branding Visual
Wednesday

Product/Service
Thursday

Industry Trivia/Fact
Friday

Featured Review
Saturday

Industry FAQ
Sunday

Reel
______

M ______________________

T ______________________

W ______________________

T ______________________

F ______________________

S ______________________

S ______________________

Snapchat has 293 million daily active users.

Dates: ______________________________

Board Name T/F

Add your title

Describe your pin

Your website

Board Name S

Add your title

Describe your pin

Your website

Mon

Tweet about your company

Tues

Tweet about a product/service

Wed

Tweet highlighting one of your online reviews

Thurs

Tweet about your industry

Fri

Tweet about something trending this week

Sat

Tweet about an upcoming sale or season

Sun

Tweet an answer to an FAQ in your industry

Weekly Hashtags ______________________________

Industry News ______________________________

Weekly Winners: MOST COMMENTS: LIKES: SHARES:

Board Name S/M

Add your title

Describe your pin

Your website

Board Name T/W

Add your title

Describe your pin

Your website

Your Account
Monday
Post about a your company

Your Account
Tuesday
Post about a product/service

Your Account
Wednesday
Post about your industry

Ideas:

Your Account
Sunday
Post a link to a blog or person you respect & your opinion

Your Account
Thursday
Post about your staff

Your Account
Friday
Post about your business logo & info

Your Account
Saturday
Post your opinion on a trending topic

Ideas:

Business Picture
Monday

Behind the scenes clip
Tuesday

Branding Visual
Wednesday

Product/Service
Thursday

Industry Trivia/Fact
Friday

Featured Review
Saturday

Industry FAQ
Sunday

Reel
______

M ________________________

T ________________________

W ________________________

T ________________________

F ________________________

S ________________________

S ________________________

38% of Instagram users have watched a video or clip on Instagram.

Dates: ______________________________

Board Name T/F

Add your title

Describe your pin

Your website

Board Name S

Add your title

Describe your pin

Your website

Mon

Tweet about your company

Tues

Tweet about a product/service

Wed

Tweet highlighting one of your online reviews

Thurs

Tweet about your industry

Fri

Tweet about something trending this week

Sat

Tweet about an upcoming sale or season

Sun

Tweet an answer to an FAQ in your industry

Weekly Hashtags ______________________________

Industry News ______________________________

Weekly Winners: MOST COMMENTS: LIKES: SHARES: ______________________________

Board Name S/M

Add your title

Describe your pin

Your website

Board Name T/W

Add your title

Describe your pin

Your website

Your Account
Monday
Post about a your company

Your Account
Tuesday
Post about a product/service

Your Account
Wednesday
Post about your industry

Ideas:

Your Account
Sunday
Post a link to a blog or person you respect & your opinion

Your Account
Thursday
Post about your staff

Your Account
Friday
Post about your business logo & info

Your Account
Saturday
Post your opinion on a trending topic

Ideas:

Business Picture
Monday

Behind the scenes clip
Tuesday

Branding Visual
Wednesday

Product/Service
Thursday

Industry Trivia/Fact
Friday

Featured Review
Saturday

Industry FAQ
Sunday

Reel
______

M ____________________

T ____________________

W ____________________

T ____________________

F ____________________

S ____________________

S ____________________

41% of Instagram users don't watch television on any sort of regular basis.

Dates: ____________________________

Board Name T/F

Add your title

Describe your pin

Your website

Board Name S

Add your title

Describe your pin

Your website

Mon

Tweet about your company

Tues

Tweet about a product/service

Wed

Tweet highlighting one of your online reviews

Thurs

Tweet about your industry

Fri

Tweet about something trending this week

Sat

Tweet about an upcoming sale or season

Sun

Tweet an answer to an FAQ in your industry

Weekly Hashtags ____________________________

Industry News ____________________________

Weekly Winners: MOST COMMENTS: LIKES: SHARES: ____________________________

Board Name S/M

Add your title

Describe your pin

Your website

Board Name T/W

Add your title

Describe your pin

Your website

Your Account
Monday
Post about a your company

Your Account
Tuesday
Post about a product/service

Your Account
Wednesday
Post about your industry

Ideas:

Your Account
Sunday
Post a link to a blog or person you respect & your opinion

Your Account
Thursday
Post about your staff

Your Account
Friday
Post about your business logo & info

Your Account
Saturday
Post your opinion on a trending topic

Ideas:

Business Picture
Monday

Behind the scenes clip
Tuesday

Branding Visual
Wednesday

Product/Service
Thursday

Industry Trivia/Fact
Friday

Featured Review
Saturday

Industry FAQ
Sunday

Reel

M ______

T ______

W ______

T ______

F ______

S ______

S ______

39% of brands spend over 20% of their marketing budget on influencer marketing.

Dates: ______________________

Board Name T/F

Add your title

Describe your pin

Your website

Board Name S

Add your title

Describe your pin

Your website

Mon

Tweet about your company

Tues

Tweet about a product/service

Wed

Tweet highlighting one of your online reviews

Thurs

Tweet about your industry

Fri

Tweet about something trending this week

Sat

Tweet about an upcoming sale or season

Sun

Tweet an answer to an FAQ in your industry

Weekly Hashtags ______________________

Industry News ______________________

Weekly Winners: MOST COMMENTS: LIKES: SHARES: ______________________

Board Name S/M

Add your title

Describe your pin

Your website

Board Name T/W

Add your title

Describe your pin

Your website

Your Account
Monday
Post about a your company

Your Account
Tuesday
Post about a product/service

Your Account
Wednesday
Post about your industry

Ideas:

Your Account
Sunday
Post a link to a blog or person you respect & your opinion

Your Account
Thursday
Post about your staff

Your Account
Friday
Post about your business logo & info

Your Account
Saturday
Post your opinion on a trending topic

Ideas:

Business Picture
Monday

Behind the scenes clip
Tuesday

Branding Visual
Wednesday

Product/Service
Thursday

Industry Trivia/Fact
Friday

Featured Review
Saturday

Industry FAQ
Sunday

Reel

M ____________________

T ____________________

W ____________________

T ____________________

F ____________________

S ____________________

S ____________________

Average users posts to their main social media platform once a day. Businesses several times a day. Great job posting all year!

Dates: ____________________

Board Name T/F

Add your title

Describe your pin

Your website

Board Name S

Add your title

Describe your pin

Your website

Mon

Tweet about your company

Tues

Tweet about a product/service

Wed

Tweet highlighting one of your online reviews

Thurs

Tweet about your industry

Fri

Tweet about something trending this week

Sat

Tweet about an upcoming sale or season

Sun

Tweet an answer to an FAQ in your industry

Weekly Hashtags ____________________

Industry News ____________________

Weekly Winners: MOST COMMENTS: LIKES: SHARES: ____________________

References

Auxier, B., & Anderson, M. (2021, April 9). *Social media use in 2021*. Pew Research Center: Internet, Science & Tech. https://www.pewresearch.org/internet/2021/04/07/social-media-use-in-2021/.

Bresnick, E. (n.d.). *Intensified PLAY: CINEMATIC study of TIKTOK mobile app*. ResearchGate. https://www.researchgate.net/publication/335570557_Intensified_Play_Cinematic_study_of_TikTok_mobile_app.

Constine, J. (2019, October 22). *Snapchat beats in Q3, adding 7M users & revenue up 50%*. TechCrunch. https://techcrunch.com/2019/10/22/snapchat-earnings-q3-2019/.

Constine, J. (2019, October 22). *Snapchat beats in Q3, adding 7M users & revenue up 50%*. TechCrunch. https://techcrunch.com/2019/10/22/snapchat-earnings-q3-2019/.

Econ King. (2021, August 6). *Full course | $60,345 in 1 month with Tik Tok ads (shopify dropshipping)*. YouTube. https://www.youtube.com/watch?v=QdTAqHvSRP8.

Environmental Protection Agency. (n.d.). EPA. http://www.epa.gov/.

Facebook Q2 2021 earnings. Facebook - Home. (n.d.). https://investor.fb.com/home/default.aspx.

Geyser, W. (2021, February 14). *The state of influencer Marketing 2020: Benchmark report*. Influencer Marketing Hub. https://influencermarketinghub.com/influencer-marketing-benchmark-report-2020/.

Ghosh, S. (2021, April 9). *10 latest social media trends that you should you follow in 2021*. Stan Ventures. https://www.stanventures.com/blog/social-media-trends-this-year/.

Gilbert, N. (2021, March 31). *5 Twitter trends for 2021/2022: Latest predictions according to experts*. Financesonline.com. https://financesonline.com/twitter-trends/.

Gwi. (n.d.). *Social media trends In 2021: Latest trends & statistics - gwi*. Social Media Trends In 2021: Latest Trends & Statistics - GWI. https://www.globalwebindex.com/reports/social.

How much time do people spend on social media in 2021? TechJury. (2021, August 5). https://techjury.net/blog/time-spent-on-social-media/#gref.

Hubspot. (n.d.). *What Your Company Needs to Know for 2020*. https://cdn2.hubspot.net/hubfs/53/HubSpotMention_ebook_2020-FINAL-1.pdf?submissionGuid=ca7c3680-5d99-4e2d-a19a-20b7aa605b8d&__hstc=20629287.26988155d4bafad489396c3f66d3e52f.1568378244734.1587070399426.1587147621240.93&__hssc=20629287.2.1587147621240&__hsfp=2793069930.

Karl. (2021, August 18). *A beginners guide to pinterest [free pdf guide]*. Dreamgrow. https://www.dreamgrow.com/a-beginners-guide-to-pinterest/.

Kemp, S. (2021, February 11). *Digital 2020: October Global STATSHOT - DATAREPORTAL – global Digital insights*. DataReportal. https://datareportal.com/reports/digital-2020-october-global-statshot.

Kemp, S. (2021, February 11). *Digital 2020: October Global STATSHOT - DATAREPORTAL – global Digital insights*. DataReportal. https://datareportal.com/reports/digital-2020-october-global-statshot.

Pierce, D. (2012, April 13). *Facebook's Instagram acquisition: The billion-dollar story*. The Verge. https://www.theverge.com/2012/4/13/2946785/facebook-instagram-acquisition.

Pinterest revenue and usage Statistics (2021). Business of Apps. (2021, July 5). http://www.businessofapps.com/data/pinterest-statistics/.

Pinterest revenue and usage Statistics (2021). Business of Apps. (2021, July 5). https://www.businessofapps.com/data/pinterest-statistics/.

Pintrest Predicts. 2021 Predictions. (n.d.). https://www.pinterest-assets.com/m/5fb1f1731fa52f72/original/Pinterest-Predicts-Report.pdf&utm_source=Site .

The power of TikTok. (n.d.). https://www.tiktok.com/business/library/the-power-of-tiktok.pdf.

The Power of TikTok. Achieving breakthrough brand building with TikTok. (n.d.). https://www.tiktok.com/business/library/the-power-of-tiktok.pdf.

Statista Research Department, & 4, A. (2021, August 4). *U.S. Snapchat users*. Statista. https://www.statista.com/statistics/558227/number-of-snapchat-users-usa/.

Swns. "Americans Check Their Phones 80 Times a DAY: STUDY." *New York Post*, New York Post, 8 Nov. 2017, nypost.com/2017/11/08/americans-check-their-phones-80-times-a-day-study/.

Social Trends 2021. Hootsuite's fifth annual report on the latest global trends in social media. (n.d.). www.tom.travel/wp-content/uploads/2020/11/SocialTrends2021_Report_en.pdf.

Twitter. (n.d.). *Summer 2021 trends on twitter*. Twitter. https://marketing.twitter.com/en/insights/twitter-conversation-report-summer-2021-trends.

Made in the USA
Las Vegas, NV
12 September 2025

27784811R10069